THE *FANTASTIC* ADVENTURES
OF PRINCE MILFRED
THE DRAGON AND THE PRINCE

This book belongs to

This is the first edition published in 2014 by Princely Press, LLC.

This, the first edition of 'The Fantastic Adventures of Prince Milfred, The Dragon and the Prince' was published in 2014 by Princely Press, LLC. (Copyright © 2014 Princely Press, LLC. - Dr. Robert Rodriguez and Kenneth Kastely)

The right of Dr. Robert Rodriguez (Author) and Kenneth Kastely (Illustrator and Designer) has been asserted by them.

All inquiries should be addressed to:
Princely Press, LLC
P.O. Box 317
Granville, OH 43023

Summary: Prince Milfred is a royal member of the Erijonia kingdom but he has a bit of a mean streak. When he encounters a flying witch and is changed into a small dragon his life changes in the best of ways.

Library of Congress Control Number: 2014903895

ISBN-13: 978-0615968896

Printed in the U.S.A.

The *Fantastic* Adventures of Prince Milfred
The Dragon and the Prince

Written by
Dr. Robert Rodriguez

Illustrated by
Kenneth Kastely

Princely Press

Once upon a time in a kingdom far, far away, there lived a little boy named Prince Milfred.

He was a beautiful little boy, and his mother and father loved him very much. The kingdom was called Erijonia.

But little Prince Milfred was also very naughty.
When the children who lived near the castle came to
play, he would chase them and call them names,
and sometimes he would break their favorite toys.
The animals and pets of the castle ran away when they
saw him because they knew that the little Prince was
so mean.

Sometimes he would pull the tails of the royal dogs
and cats, and they would run away with a "Bow wow
wow" and loud screeching "Meow". Prince Milfred liked
being mean because it made him feel bigger than he really
was and his parents just didn't know what to do.

One day the little Prince was sitting alone at the window of his bedroom high in a castle tower when he saw an approaching flock of black birds. Picking up his slingshot and some marbles, he began to shoot at the passing birds. One after another, Prince Milfred shot the marbles with all his might and some marbles came very close to the frightened little birds. The Prince thought this was really good fun. Particularly when one of his marbles hit what he thought was the biggest bird he'd ever seen...

... only it wasn't a bird at all!

What Prince Milfred
thought was a large black
bird, was in fact a witch flying
over the castle on her broomstick.

"Ouch!" cried the witch and she swooped close to the
window to see who had shot the marble. Well, the witch
was very angry; and she had heard many stories from
the people living near the kingdom of the little Prince's
naughtiness.

"It's time to teach Milfred a lesson," thought the witch,
"and do away with this nuisance forever!"

Well, as quick as you can say "Where'd he go?"
and with a little "Cat a ma zoo" the witch flew to the
castle window and turned him into a small, fat, green,
scaly dragon.

With that done, she clutched her broom
and flew away.

ZAP!

There Milfred sat looking at his scaly hands and his little, fat, thorny tail.

When the boy's mother and father came into his room they thought the little dragon had eaten their son. They were very sad AND very angry.

"Seize him!" yelled the King to the royal guards.

Quickly, the Prince, now a dragon, began to run. But right
on his thorny little heels ran the guards. Down the
winding stairs, through the courtyard and the gates
and over the castle's bridge went Milfred.

"Stop him! Stop him!" yelled the guards to the passing
people as the dragon raced by.

But the Prince was very fast, as a dragon, and headed straight for the woods. Behind him the people of the kingdom threw rocks and sticks hoping to stop the fleeing, frightened green dragon. The little Prince was very confused and very scared. Deeper and deeper he went into the woods believing the guards were right behind him.

When he finally stopped running, he was very deep in the tree crowded forest. He was pleased to have gotten away...

But he was also very lost.

At first, he was amused by the fact that he could blow long flashes of fire from his mouth and great, gray smoke rings from his nose. "Whooooosh!" he snorted, and several small branches burst into flames and then turned to ash. "Whooooosh!" again he blew and this time a small tree disappeared with a flash and a puff of smoke.

When he saw some animals approach from the distance, he snorted and bellowed; breathing hot, yellow streams of fire and sending them running back to their forest homes in fear. The little Prince laughed at seeing them so frightened.

The Prince dragon was a very scary sight. Along he went, burning small trees and branches and going even deeper and deeper into the forest.

At first, he felt safe. He thought that in only a short while he would be a boy again and find his way back home. The prince continued on deeper into the forest blowing fire at things and smoke rings in the air, but he didn't notice how very, very far into the forest he had gone.

Before long, it was beginning to get dark and he was starting to get hungry. He walked and walked and grew hungrier and hungrier. It had been quite a long time since he had seen anyone or anything familiar. He was also becoming very lonely. *"Oh I wish I could just go home and be a little boy again,"* he said to himself.

The woods grew darker and darker.

Soon he could hear strange sounds from behind the trees around him, and he grew scared.

He wished more than ever that he had behaved better and that he wasn't a dragon.

As he looked around, he noticed an owl sitting on the branch of a tree. He had always heard that owls were wise, and he thought that the owl could tell him how to become a boy again, and how to get home.

"I'm Prince Milfred," said the dragon Prince.

"Who?" said the owl, cocking its head to one side.

"Prince Milfred!" exclaimed the dragon Prince, "If you please, I know I don't look like a Prince, but I'm lost in these woods and must find my way to my home, the castle, and my mother and father."

"Who?" said the owl again, staring at the little dragon.

"My mother and father," the Prince said desperately, "The Royal Keepers of this kingdom."

"Ooooooo," Responded the owl.

"And I'm tired, and lonely, and hungry and lost. And I'm frightened by these woods!" Prince Milfred could feel himself starting to cry.

The owl looked down and said once again, "Who?"

"Who?! I am the Prince!!" Now the dragon Prince was beginning to feel angry. "I thought owls were wise. If you can't tell me the way back to the castle, can you please tell me where I can find a witch who flies on a broomstick?"

The owl said, "Who?" again.

"A witch." Milfred began to explain, "You see a terrible witch turned me into a small, fat, green dragon because I was a naughty little boy and hit her with a large marble."

Once again, the owl blinked its large round eyes and said, "Who?"

"A witch turned me into a dragon. Well, maybe I became a dragon because I was being mean to others and pulling the tails of the royal pets and shooting marbles at passing birds." The little Prince began to think, "That is, maybe I made myself into a dragon because I wasn't being very good."

With that the Prince looked into the eyes of the owl and said, "I guess owls are very wise, because now I know why the witch turned me into a dragon. And I know that if I'm ever a little boy again, I'll indeed behave much better."

With that the owl opened its great wings and flew off and the dragon Prince was again alone.

Well, now Prince Milfred was really feeling lonely, and hungry, and tired, and frightened. All he could do was walk farther and farther into the woods.

He noticed, as he walked that it was getting colder.

The wind blew the leaves on the trees, and it sounded like waves washing against a beach.

"Baahaave" Louder now, "BaaHaave!" And still the leaves rustled louder,

"BaaHaave, BaaHaave, BaaaHaaave!"

Soon Milfred began to understand the loud sound.

"BeeHaave, BeHaave, Behave, Behave!!"

As he looked up through the branches of the trees, snowflakes began to fall. All around him, ice was forming on the ground and on the leaves. The snow fell heavier and heavier. Soon everything was covered with white, cold snow. It swirled around him like horses on a merry–go–round.

Harder and harder the wind roared until he couldn't hear his own thoughts or his own sobs. The snow was getting higher and higher around the Prince dragon, and it became ever harder to walk. The grass on the ground and the lower branches on the trees disappeared under the layered blanket of snow.

It became so cold that his tears froze on the sides of his dragon nose. All he could do to keep warm was blow fire from his mouth to melt some of the snow around him.

"Fire!" he thought. "I'll build a fire!"
Quickly he began to gather leaves and twigs into a pile. "Whoooosh," he blew, but the pile was to wet to catch fire. "Whoooosh," he blew again, but all that would appear was a small dab of rising smoke. Again and again the dragon puffed flames at the little pile of leaves and sticks, but all that he could make was more melted snow and smoke.

After awhile it became very hard for him to produce even the smallest of the flames because he couldn't stop crying.

"I need some dry wood to get this fire started," said the dragon to himself. Looking up, the dragon Prince saw in the distance a very large mound of snow.

And there, out of the snow, was a long stick.

Quickly, he ran to the large pile of snow thinking that it would be good to burn the stick to keep him warm. But, from deep within the snow pile he could hear a very soft voice!

"Help!" it sounded softly.
"Help me!" He heard it again.
The voice sounded trapped and frightened.

Quickly, Prince Milfred took a deep breath and blew at the snow. But only a few sparks and smoke rings came from his mouth.

Again, he took a deeper breath and blew as hard as he could.

This time, great flames shot forth and the snow began to melt. Over and over, the dragon Prince blew his flaming breath at the snow pile until it was almost completely melted.

A strange thing happened then. As the snow melted, a dark figure began to appear. The voice continued from the figure,

"Help! Help me!"

Then from out of the snow emerged who else but the witch. "Oh no!" thought Milfred. "It's the witch! What will she turn me into now!"

But the witch knowing the good deed Milfred had done was very grateful. She realized that Milfred had learned an important lesson about being kind to others. She knew that the children of the kingdom and the royal animals would have nothing more to fear from the Prince.

And before you can say, "Where'd the dragon go?" Prince Milfred became a little boy again, and the Witch flew him home to the warm castle and to his mother and father.

From that day on, Prince Milfred never was mean to the other children or pulled the tails of the Royal pets.

He was always good and always loved.

THE END

About the Author:
Dr. Robert Rodriguez has Ph.D. degrees in Clinical Psychology and Healthcare Administration. With Master degrees in Business, Public Health, Neuropsychology, and Epidemiology. He is the author of the series 'The Fantastic Adventures of Prince Milfred'.

About the Illustrator:
Kenneth Kastely has a Bachelor of Science degree in Architectural Design. His professional and educational experience also includes Graphic Design and Illustration. He is the illustrator of the series 'The Fantastic Adventures of Prince Milfred'.

Princely Press LLC
P.O. Box 317
Granville, OH 43023

Be On the Lookout For Upcoming Adventures

www.ingramcontent.com/pod-product-compliance
Lightning Source LLC
Chambersburg PA
CBHW042125040426

42450CB00002B/68